The Ferguson Family Psalm Book

THE FERGUSON FAMILY PSALM BOOK

Michael J. McCann

The Plaid Raccoon Press
© 2023

The Ferguson Family Psalm Book is intended to accompany the original hardcover Psalm Book that is the subject of this work. Any opinions expressed herein are the author's, as are any errors reproduced from his research.

This chapbook is entirely the product of the author's hard work and creativity. No artificial intelligence applications or similar tools were used to write this book, nor will they ever be. Organically grown books are always the best!

To the pioneers:

My great-great-great grandparents
Arthur McCann and Ann Quinn

and to the memory of

Thomas Ferguson and Mary Barr,
John Stewart and Jane Buchanan,
John Ferguson and Ann Stewart,
and their descendants.

Table of Contents

Preface	9
The Book	11
The Inscriptions	13
The Story	16
The Lanark Settlers Society	16
John and Ann	17
The Children	20
The McVean Cemetery	31
The Wherefore and the Why	34
Illustrations	37
References	41
About the Author	43

Preface

I acquired the Psalm Book that is the subject of this work through an online sale in June 2021 conducted by an auction house in Smiths Falls, Ontario.

Photographs showed that the book was only in fair shape, but what attracted me to it were the numerous inscriptions on the front and back endpapers and flyleaves. They seemed to offer some interesting information related to local Lanark County history.

Antique and vintage books with religious subject matter usually don't attract the attention of many collectors, as their resale value is not exactly on a par with a first-edition Hemingway or Dickens.

I have several in my small collection, though, simply because they're old, they're attractive as books, and they have a certain sociological and historical significance that I feel should not be over-looked.

With an 1812 publication date, this book would be the oldest in my collection. The inscriptions made it impossible to resist.

As it turned out, I had a bit of a scrap with another bidder over it, and ended up winning the lot for $19.

What I brought home is worth much, much more than that.

The Book

The title page tells us that this book contains:

The
Psalms of David
In
Metre:
According to the
VERSION
Approved by the
CHURCH OF SCOTLAND,
And appointed to be used in Worship.

Edinburgh:
PRINTED BY SIR D. HUNTER BLAIR AND J.
BRUCE
Printers to the King's most Excellent Majesty

1812.

The book is bound in leather that has aged nicely over the centuries. The boards are slightly warped, the corners are rough, and the spine is damaged, so it must be graded as being in "fair" condition only.

Inside, the pages show some discolouration due to water damage that occurred in the past. Perhaps rain seeped inward from the edges when the book was being carried around outside or when it was inadvertently left out in the wagon after church.

Pages are missing from the front of the book—likely the entire first signature. The first complete psalm in the book is Psalm XV:

> Within thy tabernacle, Lord,
> who shall abide with thee?

A very good question for the Ferguson children to contemplate.

Finally, the stitching of the last signature is somewhat loose, causing it to protrude a bit. The result, no doubt, of the same wear and tear that affected the cover and removed the first signature.

The Inscriptions

Although there are no marginalia to speak of within the Psalm Book itself, the front and back endpapers and flyleaves are covered with writing, almost all of it in pen and ink. There are also a few other inscriptions in faded pencil that are difficult, if not impossible, to read.

The penmanship is cursive and seems to represent occasions when various children in the family signed their name in the book as it was passed on to them.

On the front endpaper we find:

Ann Ferguson
Ann Steward

along with a sum written in pencil and another inscription in pen and ink that's not legible.

On the front flyleaf, recto:

Ann Ferguson
Montag
Montague.

Her name is written three more times, as though she were practising her penmanship, which is quite elegant.

Front flyleaf, verso:

Thomas Ferguson
Psalm Book
Montague Twp
12th day of October
1850.

Below that is something illegible written in pencil.

On the title page, in pen and ink:

Sarah Ferguson.

At the back of the book, there are two flyleaf pages. On the first, recto:

Maggie Ferguson
Numogate Ont.

and, verso:

William Ferguson's
Book
William Ferguson
Ann Stewart

An inscription at the bottom is illegible.

On the second flyleaf at the back, recto, written in pencil:

> God Bless our Souls
> [Illegible pencil]

and verso, the most interesting inscriptions of all:

> Sarah Ferguson
> & John
> Sarah Ferguson
> Sarah Ferguson
> Book Dated the 29 of
> November AD 1866
>
> Sarah Ferguson is a good
> girl and she is the best
> in the house
>
> Mr John Ferguson
> 8th Con and 25th Lot Montague
> Smit Falls O
> Mr John Ferguson.

Finally, on the back endpaper the initials "J J." are written in ink.

The Story

The Lanark Society Settlers

In the immediate aftermath of the Napoleonic Wars, districts in Scotland such as Lanarkshire and Renfrewshire felt the pinch of an economic depression. The local weaving industry had tanked, and unemployment levels had reached a crisis point.

Emigration societies were created to raise funds in support of those wishing to depart for the New World. Sir George Ramsay, Earl of Dalhousie, was the governor-general of Canada at the time, and he arranged for settlement of Scottish families in Lanark County.

Referred to as the Lanark Society Settlers, these immigrants took up land grants in the townships of Dalhousie, Lanark, Ramsay, and elsewhere in the area.

Included among these settlers were **Thomas Ferguson** (1783-1846) and his wife, **Mary Barr** (1782-1863). They emigrated from Johnstone, Renfrewshire, to Canada with their children and settled on the east 1/2 portion of Lot 26, Concession 3, Dalhousie Township, Lanark County.

Also among the Society group were **John Stewart** (b. 1780) of Hamilton, South Lanarkshire, Scotland, and **Jane Buchanan** (1784-1854) of South Lanark. They took up land nearby on the west portion of Lot 25, Concession 2.

As it happens, our story of the Psalm Book begins with their daughter, Ann Stewart, and the son of Thomas and Mary Ferguson, John Ferguson Sr.

John and Ann

John Ferguson Sr. was born in Renfrewshire, Scotland, in June 1806. When his parents, Thomas and Mary, immigrated to Canada in 1821, he was 15 years old.

In 1830, John married **Ann Stewart**

(1809-1879), daughter of John and Janet. Their first child, John Jr., was born the following year, while they were still living with Thomas and Mary.

It would seem that the Psalm Book originally belonged to Ann, as her name was the first one written at the front of the book. Perhaps it was passed down to her from her mother.

When they left Scotland with it in 1821, the book would have been only nine years old. As I write this today, it's now 211 years old. Time is a trip, to be sure.

It's interesting to note that one of Ann's inscriptions in the Psalm Book reads "Ann Steward" while the others are all "Ann Ferguson." The former was likely written in the Psalm Book first, before she was married.

Interesting as well is the fact that she spelled it with a "d" rather than a "t." The Stewart name descended from the High Stewards of Scotland, a political office of great importance. It's said that because the "d" at the end of the Gaelic name "Steward" is pronounced like a "t," the spelling of the name changed over time.

All records of her family here in Canada, including her gravestone inscription, use the latter spelling, but it's interesting to see that Ann was aware, just the same, of her family history.

In 1832, after the birth of their first child a year before, John and Ann acquired land on Lot 24 of Concession 9, Montague Township, where they built a log shanty to raise their family. Their children included:

- John Jr. (1831-1904);
- Thomas (1833-1864);
- James (1835-1907);
- Mary (1839-1916);
- Jane Buchanan (1836-1923);
- Janet (ca. 1840-1862);
- Ann (1844-1917);
- William (1846-1864);
- Sarah (b. 1848); and,
- Margaret (1850-1934).

Ann Stewart passed away at her home on July 11, 1879, at the age of 70. She's buried in McVean Cemetery at Numogate with her parents.

John Sr. died on September 12, 1892 at the age of 85, at the home of his son James, leaving behind 37 grandchildren and 13 great-grandchildren.

According to his obituary, he lived in the log shanty all his life. For three years he worked under Colonel By in the building of the Rideau Canal, and "his funeral which took place on Wednesday afternoon last to the cemetery at Numogate was the largest in years, thus showing the high esteem in which the deceased was held."

The Children

John Jr. was born on September 24, 1831, in the log shanty in Dalhousie where his parents lived at the time with his grandparents, Thomas Ferguson and Mary Barr. He was a baby when John Sr. and Ann Stewart took up land in Montague Township and built their log home the following year on Lot 24 of Concession 9.

John Jr. wrote his name on the back endpaper of the Psalm Book, so at one time it belonged to him.

He married Elizabeth McCormick (1836-1891), and they occupied a two-storey frame structure at the intersection of County Road 15 and Ferguson Tetlock Road, on Lot 26 of Concession 8.

According to the County Directory of 1859, John Jr. owned and operated a store on the premises, and anecdotal information adds that he also started up a post office there.

On top of that, the census of 1861 lists him as a schoolteacher. He was also clerk of Montague Township, making him a very busy and important man, indeed.

He apparently coined the name "Numogate" for the hamlet by creating an anagram from "Montague."

He and Elizabeth suffered terrible misfortune with their children in the early years. A son, Wellington Ferguson, born on April 6, 1860, passed away two months later. According to the census of 1861, he died of thrush.

Another son, Robert Barr Ferguson, born August 24, 1862, died on May 25, 1864, three months from his second birthday.

As well, Annie Elizabeth, born September 7, 1865, died November 13, 1867, at the age of two.

Children who survived included John Stewart Ferguson (1862-1925); Catherine Sarah Ferguson (1867-1915); and, James Knox Ferguson (1870-1935).

John Jr. passed away on June 25, 1904 at the age of 73. Cause of death was bronchial pneumonia. He's known to be buried in the McVean Cemetery, but his marker is missing.

His wife, Elizabeth, predeceased him on July 29, 1891, at the age of 55. She's buried in McVean Cemetery with other McCormicks from her side of the family.

Thomas was born August 23, 1833. The second-oldest child, he wrote his name in the Psalm Book on October 12, 1850, when he was 17.

On January 8, 1858, he married Margaret Ann Pendergast. Their children included William John Ferguson (1861-1924) and

Ann Eliza Ferguson (1865-1893).

Thomas died on November 29, 1864, at the age of 29, before Ann Eliza was born.

James was born on October 28, 1835. He was one of the children who did not write his name in the Psalm Book.

A farmer, James was a township councillor for 20 years, and he also served as reeve.

On July 9, 1862, he married Eliza Jones. Their children included John Davis Ferguson (1863-1939), also a Montague Township reeve; Annie Jane Ferguson (1866-1934); Sarah Emily Ferguson (1868-1948); Jennie Eliza Ferguson (b. 1871); Margaret Sophia Ferguson (1873-1916); May Lydia Ferguson (1877-1932); and, James Stewart Ferguson (1881-1945).

James died March 10, 1907, and is buried in McVean Cemetery along with Eliza, who died on March 30, 1909.

Mary was born on November 7, 1839. She's another of the children who didn't write in the Psalm Book.

On March 29, 1861, she married William Tetlock (1835-1910). They had six children, including Ann Eliza Tetlock (1862-1923); Alfred Tetlock (b. 1865); William Tetlock Jr. (1867-1957); Richard A. Tetlock (1872-1950); Norman Henry Tetlock (1875-1937); and, Gilbert George Tetlock (1876-1955).

Mary passed away on February 6, 1916 and is buried with her husband's family in Drummond Township.

Jane Buchanan Ferguson was born on October 1, 1836. She was named after her maternal grandmother. She didn't write in the Psalm Book.

On June 15, 1858, she married an Irish shoemaker, Patrick Tucker of Carleton Place, son of Michael Tucker and Mary Lynde.

The census of 1861 records Patrick and Jane in Beckwith Township (Carleton Place) with their two-year-old son John J. and Jane's young brother William Ferguson, who was 14 (see below).

The 1861 census also recorded a two-year-old **J.J. Tucker** in John Sr.'s household in Numogate. Perhaps little John J. was visiting his grandparents when the enumerator arrived.

We could also guess that he was the one who wrote "JJ" on the Psalm Book's endpaper at the back.

Jane passed away on September 5, 1923 and was buried in Crams' Cemetery, now known as the Pine Grove West portion of the United Cemeteries in Carleton Place.

Janet represents a piece of guesswork, which often happens in genealogical research. She didn't write in the book.

The census of 1861 records her in her father's household, age 18, meaning she was born around 1842. We know that Jane Buchanan was already married and living in Carleton Place with her husband, Patrick Tucker, at this time, so Janet is clearly another daughter.

The only other piece of information we have for her is a headstone lying flat and broken in McVean Cemetery. The inscription reads:

In Memory of
Janet Ferguson.
Who died
Nov. 10, 1862
Aged 20 Yrs

Ann was born on May 11, 1844. She didn't write in the Psalm Book.

She married John Burns (1841-1926), and they had 10 children. She passed away on June 2, 1917 and is buried in the Franktown Public Cemetery.

William was born in 1846. At one time the Psalm Book was passed on to him, inspiring him to write in it: "William Ferguson's Book."

As we saw above, William was living with his sister Jane and her husband Patrick Tucker in 1861, when he was 14. According to the census, he was apprenticing with Patrick to become a shoemaker.

The only other reliable piece of information we have is a fragment of his gravestone in McVean Cemetery. A few years ago, someone documenting the cemetery for the *Find A Grave* website found it in the overgrowth on the far side, where it had been discarded. Only the middle portion remains. The inscription reads:

William Ferguson
Who died
Nov. 15, 1864
Aged 18 Yrs.

Sarah was born on July 12, 1848. When she wrote in the Psalm Book in 1866 she was 18 years old and no doubt still "the best girl in the house."

According to a family anecdote, her Aunt Sarah Ferguson (1819-1860), John Jr.'s sister, died a tragic death when little Sarah was 12.

Unmarried, Aunt Sarah lived with her mother, Mary Barr Ferguson, in Dalhousie. In December 1860 she'd been visiting her brother, John Jr., in Numogate. She decided on the 14th to walk home to Dalhousie, a distance of more than 60 kilometres (38 miles), so she'd be with her mother for Christmas. She never made it.

She was later found in Concession 2 of Drummond, alone in the bush, frozen to death. She was sitting on a stump with her bag on the ground beside her, having passed away while trying to rest.

She'd only covered about 16 kilometres or so of her very long journey.

Archival information from Environment Canada shows that the 14th was the coldest day of the month by far, the temperature dropping from a low of -10° Celsius (14° Fahrenheit) the day before to -21° C (-6° F). It's probable that the sudden change caught her off-guard.

Little Sarah must have been extremely upset to learn that her namesake had died such a lonely death.

As for her, it seems that Sarah has turned into the Mystery Girl of this chapbook. While all her siblings are reasonably well documented online, information related to her proved impossible to find.

FamilySearch, the genealogical website provided by The Church of Jesus Christ of Latter-Day Saints, contains an entry for her, correctly connected to her parents and siblings, but it lists a death date of 1862, which the Psalm Book tells us is incorrect. It provides no other information at all.

No headstone for her can be found in McVean Cemetery. Perhaps it was vandalized and discarded along with those of her father, her brother William, and others that have defied discovery.

In the absence of concrete details, then, little Sarah is destined to be our guiding spirit, so to speak, in this brief exploration of the Ferguson family of Montague Township. Her sunny disposition, reflected in the Psalm Book, will remind us of the buoyancy of the human spirit in the face of life's trials.

Margaret, the last child of John Ferguson and Ann Stewart connected to the Psalm Book, was born August 7, 1850. She's likely the one who wrote her name as "Maggie Ferguson/Numogate Ont."

Maggie married Donald Stewart (1839-1901), a bookkeeper, and they lived in Renfrew. Son James Arthur Stewart

(1877-1923), was a doctor; infant Annie, born in January 1879, passed away in March 1880; Margaret Eva Stewart was born 1881 and died in 1951; Jane Stewart "Jennie" (Smart) was born in 1886; and Lulu was born in 1890.

Maggie passed away on January 15, 1934 of heart disease. She was 83 years old. She's buried in the Thompson Hill Cemetery, just south of Renfrew.

The McVean Cemetery

The road intersecting County Road 15 at Numogate and running southwest to Carroll Road in Montague Township is today called the Ferguson Tetlock Road. The Canadian Pacific Railway tracks cutting across this road no longer exist, having been taken up and replaced by the Ottawa Valley Rail Trail.

On one side of the former rail line was Welsh's Station, which is no longer there. On the other side is McVean Cemetery, about 600 metres from Numogate. Walking distance.

As we've seen, many members of the Ferguson family are buried here, including several who signed their name in the Psalm Book.

When I visited the cemetery on Good Friday, 2023, the snow had just disappeared but the wind was very cold, so I dressed warmly.

I took photographs of the Ferguson and Stewart markers, then explored the far perimeter of the cemetery, which was separated from the next property by a page wire fence topped with formidable-looking barbed wire.

The margin was overgrown with lilac shoots, blackberry brambles, trees, and other tall growth. I found William's marker, where the *Find A Grave* person had kindly propped it up against a tree trunk several years ago, then went looking for others. Hoping to find Sarah's.

I found countless fragments of markers, stone obelisks piled on top of one another, and larger pieces covered with moss. Their inscriptions were worn away, lost to time.

(I also found two chunks with the inscription "Cassibo," should anyone be researching that family.)

No John Ferguson Jr., however, and no Sarah.

Many small cemeteries have suffered the same fate—vandalism, carelessness, apathy, and an unwillingness to repair and restore headstones when they were still in adequate shape to do so.

The stone bases still in the ground mark the spot were ancestors were buried, but the disappearance of their markers leaves us unable to know whose remains lie there.

It's a shame.

The Wherefore and the Why

Those of you who love books, the physical, real-world books that we can hold in our hands, may understand how I became captivated by this old, battered Psalm Book.

It has a pleasant smell—leather; dust; cloth. The pages have a high rag content, as books did back then, so they feel substantial between my fingers as I touch them, and they make a very faint crackling sound as I turn them.

The inscriptions, naturally, brought the entire thing to life, inspiring a search for the family—parents and children—who handled this book; wrote their names in it; owned it; took it to church with them; found comfort in it; passed it on.

The history of the book itself is also fascinating. Sir David Hunter-Blair, the printer/publisher, was 3rd Baronet of

Scotland. He served as a midshipman aboard the HMS *Hyacinth* before inheriting a share in an estate in Jamaica.

He also inherited the position of King's Printer for Scotland, which held a monopoly on the printing of Bibles and related publications, including Psalm Books. It was a form of political patronage, given to David's grandfather in 1785 and passed down to David's father, then to David himself.

The Psalm Book was likely purchased in Scotland and brought to Canada when Ann Stewart emigrated with her parents.

Finally, we must make note of the subject matter.

Containing all the psalms of David (minus the first 14), plus a selection of hymns at the back, it would have provided a source of hope, comfort, and guidance to the Ferguson family as they built homes for themselves, rose to prominence in the township, and suffered the loss of family members along the way.

Each child in turn would have had the

opportunity to read the psalms within it and benefit from their wisdom.

As I will try to benefit from being able to hold a genuine piece of Canadian history in my hands.

Illustrations

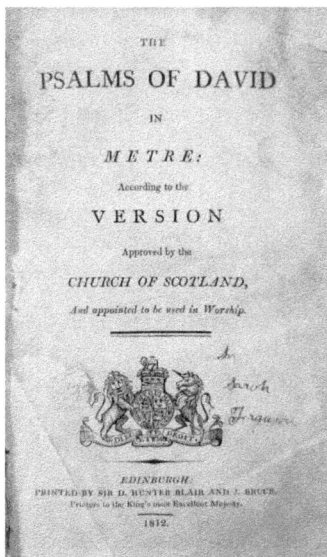

Figure 1
Psalm Book Title Page

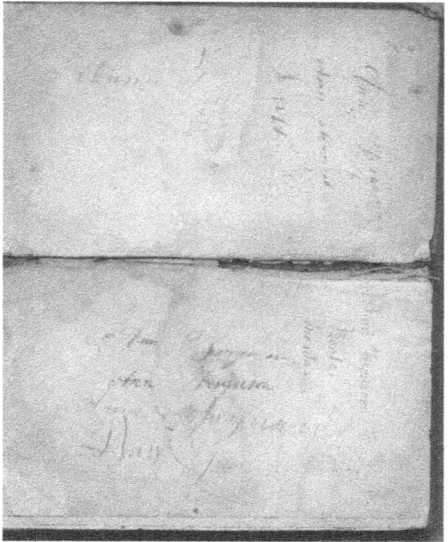

Figure 2
Inscriptions, Front
endpaper and flyleaf

38

Figure 3
Inscriptions, Back
flyleaf and endpaper

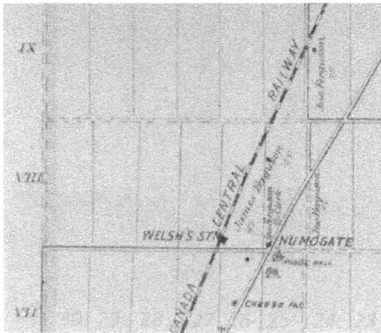

Figure 4
Detail, Montague Twp.
map, ca. 1880

Figure 5
John Ferguson Jr.
Store & Residence
Numogate, ON

Figure 8
John Ferguson Sr.

Figure 7
Ann Stewart

Figure 6
John Stewart &
Jane Buchanan

Figure 9
William Ferguson

Figure 10
The Psalm Book

References

Much of the information gathered for this chapbook was found on the *FamilySearch* website (The Church of Jesus Christ of Latter-day Saints), at ancestry.ca, and at the *Find a Grave* website.

John Ferguson Sr.'s obituary was found at: https://sites.rootsweb.com/~onlanark/NewspaperClippings/Mason/FergusonOne.htm, viewed March 28, 2023.

Stewart family origins were found at https://stewartsofbalquhidder.com/stewart-families/stewart-origins/, viewed March 28, 2023.

Information on the Lanark Society Settlers was drawn in part from E.A. McDougall, "Early Settlement in Lanark County and the Glasgow Colonial Society," *Historical Papers: Canadian Society of Church History*, 1976, 86-102. Viewed at historicalpapers.journals.yorku.ca/index.php/historicalpapers/issue/view/2262 on April 10, 2023.

For further reading, try Carol Bennett, *The Lanark Society Settlers* (Renfrew: Juniper Books, 1991).

1861 Census Canada West, Personal Census Enumeration District Eleven, Township of Montague in the County of Lanark, Public Archives of Canada, microfilmed in 1955. Viewed on March 28, 2023 at www.bac-lac. gc.ca/eng/census/1861/Pages/1861.aspx.

https://sites.rootsweb.com/~onlanark/ NewspaperClippings/Mason/FergusonOne. htm, viewed March 28, 2023.

https://www.ruralroutes.com/6381.html, viewed March 28, 2023; source of the name Numogate.

E.A. Copleston, *The Leeds, Grenville, Lanark, & Renfrew County Directory, with the Names of the Principal Inhabitants of Upwards of Seventy Towns and Villages, including the Recent Settlements on the Crown Lands, and a Variety of Useful Local Information, For the Year 1859* (Montreal: John Lovell, 1859).

Temperature data for December 14, 1860 was found at https://climate/weather.gc.ca/ climate_data/daily_data_e.html. Viewed on April 10, 2023.

Information about the publisher of the Psalm Book was found at: "Sir David Hunter-Blair, 3rd Baronet," Wikipedia.org, viewed April 2, 2023.

About the Author

Michael J. McCann lives and writes in the quiet environs of Oxford Station, Ontario. His novel *Sorrow Lake* was a finalist for the Hammett Prize for best crime novel in North America.

A graduate of Trent University (Peterborough, ON) and Queen's University (Kingston, ON), he has worked for several decades on his own family history, which by rights should be the next project on his list to complete. You'd think.

He's married to author Lynn L. Clark. They have one son.

Notes

www.ingramcontent.com/pod-product-compliance
Lightning Source LLC
Chambersburg PA
CBHW022345040426
42449CB00006B/726